MW01611859

the
Little Book
of PRAYER

Presented To:

_____

From:

_____

Published by 7 Day Systems, LLC
Austin, TX

ISBN: 978-0-9895872-1-1

Written, Edited and Designed by Knolly Williams

Available from Amazon.com and other online stores

To
My Beautiful Peet
for being my best friend
and life companion

Lord,

How can I bless You? You have endowed me with gifts and blessings beyond measure. You are my comfort and my solace. You are the passion of my existence. You are the meaning of my life.

My eyes fill with tears as I ponder Your great and magnificent love for me. You treat me as if I am the only one alive. Your attention to detail makes me smile.

I can never deserve the love You have shown me. I can never repay You for Your kindness. Alas Lord I owe You my life! It is Yours. Take it for Your good service.

I will praise You without pause or shame. You are the One I live for.

I Love You

Lord,

You hate pride. Remove it from my heart. Continue to wrap Your arms around my soul and bathe me in Your love.

I will call on You night and day. I will call on You at all times throughout the day. Make my life a song to You.

Through You I know peace; I shall not live in fear. Cast Your light before me. Illuminate my path and make my way plain.

Although the wicked are all around me, I will not be influenced by their wicked thoughts and deeds. My desire is to please You and bring You honor.

I Love You

Lord,

My heart is laid bare before You. You know all of my ways and I can hide nothing from You. Even my thoughts are exposed before You.

Lord, make me Holy. Cleanse my heart and mind. Make me pure - just like You. Prune me that I may bear the fruit that You desire. Remove the tares in my heart that the enemy has planted.

Jesus - I melt before You. Have Your way with me. Direct my thoughts and my steps. May my actions today put a smile on Your face.

I Love You

Lord,

You are glorious and magnificent. You are a mighty King! You framed the worlds with words. In the same way You frame and shape my life, when I am obedient to You. Make me malleable so that I may be used for Your good purposes.

Protect my mind from the sin that so easily ensnares me and depletes my soul. Replenish me with Your light, Your love, and Your Spirit. Show me Your mind and Your heart, and guide my steps down Your path for my life.

I Love You

Lord,

What a mighty and marvelous God You are! You bring me joy unspeakable. You bring peace, rest and calm to my spirit. How could I live without You?

Even when my soul is in despair I will praise You! When my way seems long and difficult I will lift You up. By Your grace I will acknowledge You in all of my thoughts and ways.

Your word illuminates my path. Keep me on the straight course that You have prepared before me. You ordained my steps before I was born. You orchestrated my life before I had breath. Praise Your holy name!

I Love You

Lord,

Why do the wicked forsake You? Why do they not seek Your face?

You are beautiful and Your love flows to me all the day long. I am always in Your presence. I am always in Your hand. Cradle me in Your love.

My heart responds to Your call. My feet will move swiftly to do Your work. I have determined to serve You, and I will do so all the days of my life.

Shine Your light through me today, that others may know You intimately. May my ways and my thoughts bring laughter and joy to You this day.

I Love You

Lord,

I am at a crossroads. I do not know which way to turn. You know the way; lead me Lord. Make Your way plain. Increase my understanding. Give me Your wisdom. If my life is off course, lead me back to the place where You desire me to be. True joy and happiness comes in serving You.

I have become a slave to urgent schedules. I have piled my plate high with priorities. I forsake it all for You. Clear out everything that is not in Your plan.

Direct me in the way that brings You happiness. For this Lord, I will be eternally grateful. I surrender all. Conform my will to Yours. I will obey You.

I Love You

Lord,

I will praise You in the morning. You are the God who grants sweet sleep to the Godly. May my conscience be pure before You.

What a great and majestic Lord You are. Why do You love me so? I can't comprehend Your love, yet I welcome Your embrace.

My soul cries out to You day and night. A single moment away from Your presence is agony. I cling to You and You hold me tightly.

Lord, this world is in trouble. There are distractions on every side. Men run to and fro in search of wisdom, honor and happiness. What a pitiful site. For only in You can life be complete.

I Love You

Lord,

You dwell in my heart. Please continue Your magnificent work in me, and make Your dwelling place a most welcome abode.

May my immediate answer to You always be "Yes Lord". May my actions ever be pleasing in Your sight, and may my life be in alignment with Your will.

My mind is anxious about many things. Teach me how to rest. Teach me how to watch and pray. Teach me how to be still.

Lord, still my thoughts and quiet my spirit. Make me to hear You clearly and obey Your voice. Erase my will and replace it with Yours. This is my true desire. I long to be just like You; and I long for You to be well pleased.

I Love You

Lord,

I wake up with You on my mind. Every wonderful thing I see reminds me of You. You smile at me, and I smile back.

Make me to be still and quiet. Open my eyes so that I may see Your hidden treasure all about me. Illuminate my mind and make it one with Yours.

You have turned my sorrow into joy. You dried my eyes and comforted me. Hold me close and never let me go. I sink deep into Your comforting embrace.

My soul has become one with Your Spirit. Guide me in Your everlasting ways.

I Love You

Lord,

I beseech You to direct me.

Direct my feet that they may go where You lead.

Direct my hands that they may do the work that You ordain.

Direct my mouth that it may proclaim You.

Direct my mind that all my thoughts will be subject to Your approval.

Direct my heart that it may beat in lock-step with Yours.

Live Your life through me and accomplish Your good pleasure.

I Love You

Lord,

Increase my faith. Make me to trust You with my whole heart. I lean on You completely.

Early in the morning I will rise with You at the forefront of my mind. Take over my thoughts. Lay hold of my desires. Bend and shape me to conform with Your will.

I forsake the flesh and follow hard after You. The world promised me peace, comfort, happiness and safety, but alas, those things can only be found in You.

How miserable are those who neglect You. How needy they are. It is shameful to give honor to anyone but You.

I Love You

Lord,

Direct my steps and lead my way. Fill my heart with Your joy and peace. Give me love for others. Make me a light that shines for You everywhere I go.

Thank You for designing me. Continue to fashion me—make me a perfect object of obedience and allegiance to You.

You are worthy of much more than I could possibly give. Even so, all that I have is Yours. Take and use me as You see fit.

I Love You

Lord,

Your ways are just. I trust You implicitly and I trust You with my whole heart. I am so grateful for Your salvation.

I remember well when I was lost without You. I had traveled deep into a cavernous abyss and lost my way. Deeper and deeper I traveled, until nothing around me was recognizable. I was in darkness.

Finally, when I became weary of worshiping myself, I cried out to You. How quickly You heard my cry! You snatched me from that deep pit and enveloped me in Your love. Yes, I will eternally be grateful for Your wonderful salvation. My hear is Yours and I shall never return to darkness. I will bathe in Your light.

I Love You

Lord,

I am Your masterpiece. You created me for Your good pleasure and for Your purposes. I will follow Your leading.

The trees in the forest raise their hands to praise You. I will too. The flowers in the fields stretch forth to receive Your light. I will do the same. Everything in nature is Your handiwork and a reflection of Your divine character. How blessed I am to be among the living!

Continue to do Your mighty restorative work on my heart. Prune me today that I may bear the fruit that You desire. May I not resist Your work in my life. It is necessary in order for me to become like You.

I Love You

Lord,

Continue to do Your mighty restorative work on my heart.

Above all things Lord, please grow the fruit of Love in my life. I desire to love the way You love. I desire to see the way You see. Make me to care deeply for others and despise the material things of this world.

There is much work yet to be done in my life Lord, but I lay myself on Your surgical table. Gently remove all traces of me that exist and replace them with You. May I be pleasing in Your sight.

I Love You

Lord,

A new day brings new praises to You! More reasons to praise Your Holy name!

Today, make my life an imitation of Christ's. Turn my mind and heart away from carnal things. May I despise the temporal and long for the eternal.

My God, I treasure You. You are high and lifted up. I put no other gods before You! You alone are worthy of my worship and allegiance. I am Your soldier and I march boldly forward in Your name and for Your cause.

I shall not fear slander or death. I will serve You in sickness and in health. May I continually live and dwell in the center of Your will.

I Love You

Lord,

You are wonderful! Your ways are perfect. Your love is the limitless.

Teach me how to praise You perfectly. Teach me how to appreciate Your goodness. Teach me how to share Your love.

I look forward to the home that You have prepared for me. There I will praise and serve You day and night. Let me begin the work here. Let me share Your light and love with others. Use my hands, feet and my heart to accomplish Your work.

I trust completely in You. I lean wholly on Your understanding. May I acknowledge You in everything I do and say.

I Love You

Lord,

Today, give me good success. Envelop me in Your presence. Keep my feet on Your path.

Make me to notice Your reflection all around me. Help me to pay attention to Your promptings. Lord, I submit myself to You completely.

You are the great and mighty King! To You alone belong all praise, honor and glory—forever and ever! I will trust no other.

May I not hesitate to follow Your commands. Tame me.

As long as I have You, I have need of nothing. You supply all of my needs.

I Love You

Lord,

Your children cry out to You day and night - and You hear our cries! Whom shall I fear? Of whom shall I be afraid? I will praise You all the day long. I will trust You with all that is within me. Truly it is a disgrace to distrust the Almighty.

I own no earthly goods. Everything is Yours. Use it to accomplish Your work.

I have no earthly cares. I have cast them all on You. Handle them according to Your will. Lord - all of my troubles, cares and struggles I turn over to You. I will carry them no more. They are no longer mine.

I Love You

Lord,

It is such a privilege to be part of Your family. You are so worthy to be praised! You are the great and priceless Pearl. I am so happy that I found You. You pursued me. You overtook me. And now I am completely Yours.

Lord, remove my anxiety. Take away my doubt. Exile my fears. I do trust You completely. I yield to Your will.

My whole heart, mind and soul is lifted up to You. You are an awesome and Holy Redeemer. How I long to be just like You!

I Love You

Lord,

See now, I lay broken and crumbled before You. My own will has been shattered. My own desires have been abandoned. I forsake it all for the cross of Christ. I lay it all down at Your feet.

Lord, take my gifts and talents and use them according to Your purposes. Lead me where You want me to go.

Lord let us dine together. You are so romantic. Please, I pray, make me like You. May I think with Your mind. May I see with Your eyes. May I work with Your hands. May I travel with Your feet.

You are in me and I am in You. We are inseparable.

I Love You

Lord,

As I wander through the paths of life that You set before me, may I ever be mindful of Your love for me. Help me to love others perfectly.

Make my meditations to You be pure and uncontrived. Cleanse the impurities of my heart. Make me to reflect You. Still my spirit.

Open my eyes today that I may see things the way that You see them. Give me Your sweet peace.

Your presence and Your love is all I desire. Remove the love of worldly things from heart. Make me just like You.

I Love You

Lord,

How I long for Your embrace. But alas - You are within me! I don't have to look out-wardly for You. You dwell inside of my heart and You have captivated my soul.

You bring me joy unspeakable. Though the world around me be shaken, I will rest in the promise and assurance of Your love. In Your word I find wisdom.

You are a sweet aroma to me. May I never loose the scent of Your fragrance. Continue to fashion me into the miracle that pleases You.

I Love You

Lord,

You are majestic. Lord You are righteous. Lord You are Holy. Lord there is none like You.

Although I feel unworthy, I will praise You anyway. I will not allow the enemy to steal my joy. I will worship You.

The cares of this world continually try to rob me of Your peace. The duties of this life encroach on my duties to You. Oh how I welcome Your grace!

My priority is Your will. Nothing else matters to me.

I Love You

Lord,

I thank You for this new day; a new opportunity to praise and serve You! Go before me this day. Prepare the way, and have Your way with me.

The enemy prepares a snare and a trap for me. Go before me, and confound the plans of he who conspires against me.

You are the Vine and I am but a branch. Thank You for Your pruning work in me. Continue to grow the fruits of the Spirit within me. Make this branch a pleasant sight in Your garden.

Wherever I go, You are here. That brings me comfort. That brings me great joy.

I Love You

Lord,

I am so broken and needy. My failures are many. I continue to miss the mark. I stumble repeatedly.

With a contrite spirit, I fall into Your arms. I melt into Your grace. Shield and cover me.

I will sound loud the trumpet! I will shout upon the rooftops! For I received Your grace, and my heart and soul are healed. How precious is my quiet time with You.

I long for my glorified body and my incorruptible heart.

I Love You

Lord,

You are to be treasured above all else. You are the Holy One. Your flame burns bright, and is never extinguished.

Lord, turn my mind and heart away from worthless things. Make me desire You always. Fill my heart with compassion for others. Silence the distractions of this world, so that I may focus on You.

My heart tries to grow cold. My sins try to well up within me. My fears encamp round about me. Lord, You are my comfort. I run to You. I snuggle in Your arms.

I Love You

Lord,

Make a clear path before me. Show me the way to go. Make me to walk in Your righteousness.

When my flesh lays ahold of me, You will prevail. Today I give You my life and my allegiance.

Your Spirit abides in me. He is my everlasting comfort. He bears witness against my impure motives. He stands ready to do His supernatural cleansing work in me. May I not resist Him.

I Love You

Lord,

You are my abiding treasure! I am so lost without You. My soul hungers and thirsts for Your Spirit.

Lord - where can I go to hide from You? You know all of my ways. You know my innermost secrets. You know my longings and desires. You know my hurts and pains. You know my needs. Although I will never truly know myself, You know me.

There is sweet comfort in surrender to the Lord. When I am in Your will I am at peace. I can relax. I am at rest.

I Love You

Lord,

Wow! You are the Mighty One—The Ancient of Days! You are the Creator of the heavens and the earth. You are the Redeemer of my soul. Even so, You long to spend precious moments with me. Yes, precious and tender are the moments we two can share!

All the day long we walk hand-in-hand. Do not allow me to escape from Your presence. Hold me tightly. Never let me go.

I am so in love with You Jesus. Words only have the capacity to express a fraction of my true love and desire for You. I am completely enraptured in You.

Lord, keep me pure and clean. Keep all false idols far from me. You are my idol.

I Love You

Lord,

Why am I so deaf to Your voice? Make me to hear You clearly. I desire to be obedient to You. I want my life to be a song; constantly singing praises to You.

You rescued me from darkness and depravity. You have set me in a place of honor. Why so? While I deserve death, You have given me live.

You ransomed me and called me back to You. I will use all of eternity to sing Your praises. You have captured my heart. You possess my mind.

I Love You

Lord,

In You rests all my hopes and dreams. You direct my present, and my future is safe in Your hands. I will not worry or fear. Instead I turn to You.

My soul hungers for You. Lord I am weary with trying to figure things out. You know the way. Show me what You see.

Lord I pledge to walk in Your will all the days of my life. Abide in me so that I may live and please You. Take away my stubbornness and soften my stiff heart. I want to make You happy.

The more I see into my own heart the more I see how profoundly I need You. I am holding on to You and I shall never let go. You alone are my source of joy.

I Love You

Lord,

I am prone to drift away from You. I do this because my own heart betrays me. It looks elsewhere for the love and companionship that can only be had in You.

Make me steady. Make my desire for You overtake me. You make me completely happy.

The sunshine and the rain both praise You. You are the Creator of all things. How delightful You are!

In times of joy and triumph, I will praise You. In times of great sorrow, I will praise You.

I Love You

Lord,

I long to abandon wickedness. Turn my heart away from worthless things. I cry out to You in agony! My soul is vexed. My disobedience and my sinful heart grieves me bitterly.

Lord, I offer myself as a living sacrifice for Your service. Use me in all ways pleasing to You. Make me think with Your mind, and make me act with Your will. I am Your lover and Your servant. Jesus - use me to Your glory. May I bring You comfort.

Teach me to be patient and humble. Continue to mold me in Your image. Equip me for Your work. Enlighten me and show me Your will.

This is the day that You have made – I will rejoice and be glad in it!

I Love You

Lord,

You are a strong and mighty Fortress. I will run to You for refuge. I will lean on You for my strength. You are my shelter.

I praise You for the wonder of a new day. Fulfill Your will. Shape and mold me. Glorify Your name.

Everything in nature sings Your praises. My heart and soul cries to You.

Continue to lead me in Your everlasting ways. Preserve my heart and soul for Your service and use.

My God - You are not meant to be described with words. When I allow Your spirit to meld with my soul—mortal words escape me. I am silenced.

I Love You

Lord,

Life is so lonely without You. How can anyone desire a life apart from Your presence? You are a great and mighty miracle. You have changed me completely. I will praise You day and night for what You have done for me.

The enemy has once again encamped around me. He attempts to entice me with the ways and the entrapments of the world. But this world is shattered and corrupt. It has nothing good to offer me. My home is Heaven.

Oh how I will beam when I stand outside the mansion You have prepared for me. And when I make my home in the new Jerusalem, it is there that I will praise You forever.

I Love You

Lord,

You knew me before You created time. Thank You for the most bountiful and precious gift of life. Hold me close and never let me go.

You laid down Your life so that I may live. Now I lay down my life so that I may live in You.

All of creation praises Your name. I join in with praises that well up from the bottom of my heart.

Make me to know Your will. Grant me the gift of obedience. You are my everything.

I Love You

Lord,

What great and mighty promises You have given me! You keep every one of them.

Lord You alone are worthy of all praise, honor, respect and glory. May I render my portion to You this day.

You are the Holy of Holies—yet You love spending time with me. Make me to desire to spend quality time with You. Make my entire life revolve around You.

Make me to be pure of heart and slow to speak. Make me to reflect Your love.

You are the greatest gift. You bring joy to my soul and rest to my weary bones. Arrest my flesh. Enrapture me. Captivate my mind. Soften my heart.

I Love You

Lord,

You are the love of my life. I long to stroll with You hand in hand, in the new Jerusalem. I will love and serve You all the days of my life.

In the midst of dark days, I shall not be moved. You love spending time with me. Make me to love Your presence just as much.

Jesus, You alone are worthy of my loyalty and love. Make me to love You completely. Make me to lay down my life for Yours. Replace my will with Your will. Accomplish Your work in me.

I thank You for what You have made me to be. I thank You that I am not what I could have become. You are worthy of more than I can give. Make me to give my all.

I Love You

Lord,

You are my light and my life. Change my priorities. I will praise You even when I don't feel like it. Giving glory and honor to You brings joy to my soul. You refresh me.

Though I am like a leaf tossed about by the wind, You reach out and gently guide me. When I have no sense of direction, You are always there to show me the way.

You gave up Your life for me. May I have the courage to give up my life for You.

Everything that I could ever hope for comes from You. My desire is to fulfill Your will.

I will worship You without fear, shame or guilt.

I Love You

Lord,

You are my found treasure. You banish all of my fears. You bring peace to my soul. I will not look to another for my answers. You alone are the source of my wisdom. I am safe when I am with You.

Purify my heart and make it like Yours. Make me to meditate on the things that You meditate on. Make me to love the things that You love.

Clear my mind of all the meaningless distractions that brazenly attempt to assert their position of priority. Nothing is important unless it is sanctioned by You.

Give me the wisdom to understand and follow Your will.

I Love You

Lord,

You are the God who loves me and heals me. You are my Redeemer. My love for You grows with each passing day. Make this day most special.

Exchange my calamity for calm. Take away my pride and give me Your peace. Replace my weariness with Your rest.

My allegiance is to You alone. I will love You all of my days upon the earth, and I will reign with You forever.

Make me to be the malleable clay that You can readily work with. Mold me into the object of Your fascination. I will meditate on You both day and night. I will praise Your holy name.

I Love You

Lord,

You are a gorgeous and most beautiful rose. I dream about You all throughout the day and night. You consume my thoughts and my life. Your love consumes me like a blazing fire.

You occupy the innermost recesses of my being. You know me.

You have made my yoke easy and my burdens light. Still my mind and quiet my thoughts.

Today, let us romp and play together! Oh, how You love me! Grow my love for You Lord. I commit to You my loyalty and allegiance. I present myself to You as Your sweet and fragrant living sacrifice. Use me as You see fit.

I Love You

Lord,

Let me tap into You. I want to know Your thoughts. I want to be in alignment with You. Your will is all that matters.

When I open my eyes in the morning I see You. When I close my eyes in the evening I see You. You give me life and You give me sweet rest.

Working for You is a most magnificent honor. Use me as You see fit. I am truly blessed to be counted among those whom You know.

Quiet my chaotic mind so that I may focus on You. My priority is Your will.

I Love You

Lord,

You are my refuge. I will hide myself in Your love. This new day brings new challenges which I eagerly await. You walk before me.

I am the object of Your affection and You are the love of my life. May I not be distracted by worthless, earthly things.

Please transform my heart and my mind. Make me an obedient servant. I only want to do what is in Your best interests.

O how I thoroughly despise the carnal side of my nature. Please continue to carve out the flesh that dwells within me. Purify me Lord. Yes! I am ever grateful for Your grace.

I Love You

Lord,

I praise You. You are the God who parted the seas so that Your children could walk safely through. You are the God who calmed the storm, so that Your disciples could enjoy safety and peace.

Today I thank You for all of the seas that You have parted in my life. I thank You for all of the storms that You have calmed in my soul.

Lord, teach me how to love You. Teach me how to praise You. Teach me how to serve You. I want to know You the way You want to be known.

I Love You

Lord,

I am fascinated by You. Your majesty holds me spellbound. Make me to love You more.

Prepare my heart and soul for my eternal home. Oh how I look forward to our future together. How I long to gaze into Your eyes while You hold me close.

I am the passion of Your heart. You are my reason for living. Your love for me is altogether overwhelming. My mind cannot comprehend it.

Empty me of myself so that I may experience more of You.

I Love You

Lord,

You are my rock. You are my constant Companion. You are my Lover. My heart dances when I think of You. I pause frequently to reflect on Your amazing love and kindness towards me.

Please protect me from anything that is not beneficial. Hold me close and rock me gently. I am cuddled up in Your arms of love. Hold me tighter than You ever have before.

Your wisdom is life. Your guidance is the path of life. I embrace everything that You are, and I eagerly reach out for more of You.

I must decrease so that You may increase. Crucify my flesh. Remove all traces of me so that You are all that remains.

I Love You

Lord,

I desire the abundant life that You promise. I want to completely surrender to You. I desire to completely trust You. I put all my hopes, desires and dreams in Your hands. You are the Master of my future.

You give me the most refreshing peace and rest. My faith in You grows stronger with each passing day. I see You at work everywhere I look. I also can see You at work within my heart.

Lead me, guide me, and make me to follow. Place my feet on the path that leads to joy unspeakable. I am Yours.

I Love You

Lord,

You have made my heart a flower garden. You plant the most beautiful flowers, boasting the most spectacular colors. You gently remove the weeds, and tend its grounds on a regular basis. You trim and prune as needed, and You water regularly. Make the grounds of my heart fertile so that it may spring forth with abundant praises to You. Today, I give You Lordship over my entire life. Use my tongue to Your honor and glory.

Lord, how bright You shine! How I long to stand in Your presence. Oh how I thank You for dwelling within me. Lead and guide me in Your perfect way.

I Love You

Lord,

You have promised to never leave me nor forsake me. You have kept Your word. I am comforted by Your presence. I shall not put my trust in any other.

I am never alone - for no matter where I am - there You are. Thank You my God for this wonderful promise.

I am completely inadequate and unworthy. Nevertheless You love me. Without You I am nothing. With You I am complete.

There is nothing so small or insignificant that I would not look to You for guidance. You orchestrate my life.

My desire is to stay in the center of Your will and in the palm of Your hand.

I Love You

Lord,

You are so refreshing. I can't imagine life without You. Grant me Your peace today. I want to know You more intimately.

Give me a deeper understanding of Your presence. Help me to see You in the opportunities and people that I come in contact with. Make me to be a blessing to You.

Give me the courage to move out in faith. Give me the strength to act on Your behalf. Give me the desire to follow You.

You are more wonderful than words can articulate. You are wisdom and love and grace. You are the love of my life. I treasure my time with You now, and I look forward to our endless future together.

I Love You

Lord,

To know You is the great ambition of my life. To please You is my singular purpose. To reflect You is the greatest honor. You are my priority.

Make me available for Your good pleasure. Grant me time to spend with You. Make me to love You. Give me Your character.

I thank You for the gift of immortality. I will rule and reign with You forever. You alone have given me life. Because of You I shall never see death.

What in this life is so important that I neglect You? Nothing in this life matters more than You. Nothing in the universe matters more than You. Your will is all there is.

I Love You

Lord,

My love for You grows like a raging fire. I will proclaim Your name with fervor and zeal. Keep me forever in Your way.

I have tasted the truth and can live by nothing else. Continue Your cleansing work in my life. Purify my heart and renew my mind. Make my life reflective of Your desires.

You care for me deeply. Make me to care for You. Your love is a deep ocean, and I will experience it forever.

When I lie down to sleep You make my rest sweet and enticing. My burdens You gladly bear, and my sorrows are swallowed up in Your joy.

I Love You

Lord,

My heart is filled with gratitude for Your loving kindness. I am in awe when I consider Your majesty and great wisdom. You care for me dearly.

When I am in trouble You are there to help me. When I fall You are there to catch me. When I laugh You laugh with me. And when I cry, You wipe away my tears.

You are the bright Morning Star that shines throughout my day. My heart is filled with gratitude for all of Your bountiful blessings.

How special and wonderful it is to be loved by You. Let Your light shine through me. Give me the courage to stand for You.

I Love You

57

Lord,

You are the lighthouse that shines brightly and guides me safely to my destination. You have earned my complete and total trust. I am loyal to You alone.

Your way is wonderful, and the outcome of all matters rests safely in Your hands. I will take joy in not knowing. I will find peace in trusting You to make the right choices and decisions for me.

I will walk with You closely, so that I may hear Your still small voice. Give me the courage to act in accordance with Your will.

I Love You

Lord,

You are the song of my heart. You are my joy. I am so happy that I know You.

Deepen my desire for intimacy with You. Make my love for You grow stronger with each passing day.

Replace the troubles of my heart with Your peace. Calm my racing mind and make my soul relax.

You are the Rock that I cling to. You are my comfort. Your words are sure, and Your way leads to life. I look forward to spending eternity with You!

I Love You

Lord,

You alone are majestic and mighty. You are my covering and my protection. I trust You completely. Your kingdom is my primary concern.

All of heaven moves at the sound of Your voice. Make me to move when I hear You speaking. The angels attend to Your desires without question. Give me the obedience of angels.

Help me to laugh with those who laugh and mourn with those who mourn. Give me a genuine love for my fellow man. Make me to see them through Your eyes and love them as You do.

I Love You

Lord,

Why do I allow my imagination to run away with me? Only You know the end from the beginning, and I know that my future rest safely and securely in Your hands.

Today I surrender my imagination to You. I also hand You all of my fears and my anxiety. I also give You my need to know. My only agenda is Your will.

You are the great and wonderful Creator God, and my journey with You is most pleasurable and exciting. I will not spoil the surprise by trying to look ahead.

You have given me all that I need from day to day. Help me to make Your kingdom my primary concern.

I Love You

Lord,

You center me. In a rushed and hurried world, You bring me peace and calm. You quench my thirst. You belay my fears.

Why should I worry when You command me not to? I believe that You are in control, and I will act accordingly.

Nothing in this life can separate me from You; and death only brings me closer to You. What then shall I fear?

Even when the sky begins to fall and the earth beneath my feet begins to crumble, I will stand confident in You. You are my safety.

I Love You

Lord,

You have anointed me to preach Your Gospel; the good news of Your kingdom. What an awesome privilege. Help me to know You fully so that I may represent You rightly.

Your light shines upon me wherever I am. When dark despair begins to encroach me, Your light floods in. You are my joy.

Thank You for Your loving kindness. You are ever mindful of me. You watch over me and care for me tenderly and personally.

I will boldly and blindly follow You wherever You lead. Though I don't understand, nor do I comprehend what You are up to, still I will follow. Life with You is an adventure and I will relax and enjoy the journey!

I Love You

Lord,

I am eternally thankful for Your grace. Even when my days seem dark and lonely, You are here with me, ever present.

How can I ever turn away from You? You are my everything. You are my hope, and I can run to no other.

My mind is captivated by the dreams of Your heart. Though to others it may appear that I am roaming and wandering, You are, in fact, leading me and guiding me to Your destinations.

I will not doubt You. I will believe. My heart burns with excitement and anticipation as the journey unfolds!

I Love You

Lord,

My heart is filled with joy and gratitude because of Your awesome and amazing love. My soul longs to reflect Your character.

Life is filled with a great many distractions. I will not let the noise of this world crowd out my time with You.

Your work of pruning in my life is often painful. Sometimes You simply clip here and there. Other times You trim me way back – almost to the ground! In either case it is to my benefit. Your pruning allows me to grow the big, beautiful, luscious fruit that I was meant to bear.

My dear God - having You in my life is indeed a miracle that I am eternally grateful for. You're the best.

I Love You

Lord,

Today I choose joy. Regardless of my current circumstances, I will remain mindful that You are in control. I will not worry about the past, nor will I fret about the future. I will take the time to be present and in the moment.

Oh how You love me! You never tire or grow weary of me. You exchange my faults for Your grace. Your forgiveness knows no bounds and Your love has no end. I will serve You, for You have completely won me over.

You have ordered my life and all I need do is follow in Your footsteps. You lead me safely and carefully. You lead me with exuberance and excitement. I will enjoy the journey.

I Love You

Lord,

You are majestic and wonderful. Your glory and might spreads out to eternity.

I am in awe of Your magnificence. Your beauty is beyond compare. You reveal Yourself to me every day.

Your love for me is deeper than any ocean. Your love looks beyond my biggest faults. Even when I forsake You, Your love endures.

I am Yours forever. Use me as an instrument of Your divine purpose and will. I will follow You wherever You lead.

I want to bring You joy and pleasure. When my feet lead astray, gently guide me back to the right path. And, at times, carry me safely to my destination in Your mighty arms of love.

I Love You

Lord,

Guide me down the path that leads to life, and leads to You. I have tried my own way and failed. Only You know what is best for me.

The more I focus on You, the better I hear Your voice. May the distractions of this world not pull me away from You!

I am Yours forever and You are mine. You bring me the comfort I am looking for. You give me the peace and contentment I seek.

Longing for that which You do not desire for me is futile and destructive. Change my desires to align with Your will. My greatest desire is to see You well pleased.

I Love You

Lord,

Your glory fills both the heavens and the earth. You are magnificent and worthy of my continual praise. As I reflect on Your wonderful way towards me, my heart is filled with gratitude.

My love for this world decreases with each passing day; and my love for You increases proportionately. Replace my greed with contentment.

Teach me to continually seek Your guidance in all matters. For only You know the safe route which will lead to the best outcome.

I acknowledge that I am but a child in need. You alone can fulfill every need and every desire of my heart.

I Love You

Lord,

Your knowledge and wisdom is without end. I will always seek You for every decision in my life, because only You know the right way.

You are the Creator of all there is. You are truth, and Your ways are perfect. I will love and adore You forever.

When I look up at the night sky I think of You. When I observe the trees, hear the birds in song, and see flowers in bloom, I think of You. You have captivated my mind, body and soul.

You are worthy of my best. I owe it to You to be the best I can be and to live a life with no regrets. Continue to gently mold me into what I ought to be.

I Love You

Lord,

I am Your servant. I await Your instructions and I pledge to do Your will. You always bring me joy.

Even when things don't seem to go my way, I will praise You. When times are hard, I will praise You. When the journey becomes arduous, still I will praise You. You will never give me more than I can bear.

You are the greatest gift I could wish for. You are the gift that keeps on giving. How truly blessed I am!

I am a citizen of Your kingdom. I am a sheep in Your flock. I live to bring You glory. My greatest desire is Your presence.

I Love You

Lord,

How exceedingly glad I am to have You in my life! You are my Guide. Without You I am absolutely nothing.

I treasure and desire intimacy with You. You are my love and affection. You have a magnificent design for my life. I will follow Your plan.

I will see every challenge in life as an opportunity. Adversity brings opportunity for me to learn and grow. Adversity brings me humility. Adversity helps mold me into Your image.

I thank You for all things and I will be joyful and exceedingly glad, as You command. Grant me Your grace and Your power to live as You desire.

I Love You

Lord,

Mortal words cannot express how magnificent You are. My praises are reserved only for You. You are the wonderful light that glows throughout my soul.

You have refreshed me and renewed my mind. At the thought of You my soul leaps for joy.

I will follow Your command and I will not worry about my life or my future. Both are secure and safe in Your capable hands.

With You as my Guide I am confident and sure. My hope is in You - and You never disappoint.

I Love You

Lord,

You are majestic and magnificent. You are crowned and clothed in glory. How wonderful it is to know You.

You considered me when You formed the worlds. I was on Your mind even before You created the angels.

When You spoke everything into existence I existed in Your mind, and You knew me. It is a privilege and an honor to recline at Your table.

Although I do not completely understand Your ways - I will trust You, for You are completely trustworthy. My life, my existence and all that I possess are Yours to do with as You please.

I Love You

Lord,

You are my strength. You are the rock that I can always count on. I cling to You.

Without You nothing has meaning. Without Your love this world is cold and empty.

I long for the endless days that we will spend together. Eternity with You is the prize I am racing for.

Fill my head with the things that are meaningful to You. May I abandon my ways and exchange my habits for Yours.

I Love You

Lord,

You are my morning flower. I am so in love with You. I will lift You up and praise Your name forever.

You are the rarest gem - beautiful in every way. Your amazing wonders never cease.

You illuminate the path beneath me so that my feet cannot slip. You direct each step I take.

You never hide Your face from me. You are ever present. You are my constant companion. What an honor it is to walk with the Creator of the universe!

I Love You

Lord,

I cling to You. There is no place I would rather be than in Your presence.

You are my first thought in the morning and my last thought every evening. All through the day I think of You and converse with You.

I am in awe at the magnificent work of Your hands. How marvelous and wonderful You are!

You are holy, powerful and mighty - yet You humble Yourself for my sake. All of nature sings Your praises and I am at the forefront of that majestic chorus!

I Love You

Lord,

You are magnificent and beyond compare. Help me to understand and appreciate the great value of Your kingdom.

You have blessed me with peace beyond all understanding and the abundant life You promised in Your word. It is my prayer that I can honor You and bless You with all that I am, and all that You have given.

You illuminate my journey as I trek through this treacherous world. Without You as my guide I would surely be wasting away in a pit.

You have given me hope and have promised me a bountiful future. Your love has won me over and I am Yours forever.

I Love You

Lord,

You are my solace. My heart is Your throne and You rule ever so justly.

You take care of my every need. I will never cease to be amazed by Your love, wisdom and ingenuity.

When I ponder all the things You have created, I am overwhelmed. You have made me so delicate and unique.

I am so happy to be called by Your name. Even when You abolish time, I will continue to live and love You... forever.

I Love You

Lord,

You are marvelous, wonderful and spectacular! Nothing is impossible for You. Nothing is beyond the scope of Your capabilities.

I will trust in You with my entire being. I give myself to You without reservation.

Your love and Your presence has brightened my life. I accept whatever lot You have for me - I will be cheerful and I will not complain.

Keep me in Your perfect way and on Your perfect path. Use me for Your glory wherever I am.

I Love You

Lord,

I am continually drawn to You. When I am tired and weary, You energize me with Your love.

My hope is in You alone and You never disappoint. In Your time You make all things lovely and beautiful.

You turn my weeping into praising and my sorrow into joy. You lead and guide me as I wander through this treacherous world.

I will keep my mind fixated on You and my heart in tune with Yours. As I complete my journey, I will walk only down the paths that You have laid out before me.

I Love You

Lord,

Your great love for me is overwhelming. Every day You demonstrate how deeply You care for me.

You comfort me when I am in despair. You never forget me, for You are my constant companion.

Some days seem unbearable - nearly impossible to get through. But I am reminded that You are near.

You shower me with Your love and kindness, and You lead and guide me in the perfect way. Because You are my guide, I shall never be afraid.

I Love You

Lord,

I thank You for Your loyalty. You have been faithful to me, even when I have been unfaithful to You. You have shown me more loving kindness than I could have ever imagined existed.

You alone are my hope. I am content. You have given me everything I need. Your promises are true, and You keep them faithfully.

My burning desire is to know You and to please You. I completely surrender my will to You.

Show me Your perfect way and I will walk in it. Give me the full measure of Your strength, so that I may overcome the enemy and live for You.

I Love You

Lord,

You are a most wonderful and gracious God. I want to serve You fully. I adore You.

When I survey the land, the seas, the skies and all that is around me, I am overwhelmed by Your creativity. How thrilled I am that You are my God!

I choose to hold Your hand and walk side-by-side with You. I will let You lead the way. And when I am weary, I will let You carry me.

I will continue to cling tightly to You. My heart melts like wax and leaps for joy at the sound of Your name.

I Love You

Lord,

I praise and magnify Your name! You are a just and holy God. You are the only one who truly cares for me.

I will pay no heed to the slanderous words of others. You are a righteous judge and I look to You alone for approval.

My soul cries out for more of You. You relieve me of my cares and worries. No matter what this life brings, I will cling to You.

I will honor You with my life. I will trust You to make the best decisions for me. I will serve You and remain faithfully Yours forever.

I Love You

85

Lord,

I honor You. You alone are worthy of my deepest devotion, admiration and praise.

I empty myself of me so that I may be filled with You. I want Your Spirit to be the driver in my life. Making decisions without You is not an option for me.

Make me to serve You fully. I want to dedicate my time and attention to Your will. I want to fulfill Your desires.

You alone know the right paths for me. You have preordained the way in which I should walk. Guide me safely along my way.

I Love You

Lord,

How thrilling it is to be Your student. The more I keep my eyes on You, the more I learn and the clearer I see.

You are utterly remarkable. Everything around me was either made by You or built from materials You provided. Who else could I turn to when I am in need? You alone hold the keys to ultimate wisdom and knowledge.

You know me intimately and completely – down to the finest detail. You know what is best for me. You have numbered the hairs on my head and my days on this earth.

I pledge to give You all of me, not just my leftovers. My mind, body and soul are Yours to do with as You wish.

I Love You

Lord,

I appreciate You. Whenever I feel alone You are here with me. Whenever I am in need, You come through for me. Whenever I am hurting, You bring me comfort.

I am always at the forefront of Your mind. You give me Your undivided attention. Your watchful eye doesn't miss a single thing. You are intimately involved in the big and small things of my life.

You are irreplaceable. Though I have often tried to fill the void in my heart with other things, I have come to realize that nothing can replace You.

For You, I lay down my life. Pick it up and make it into something that pleases You and brings You joy.

I Love You

Lord,

Thank You for the many gifts that You have blessed me with. I pray that I will always use them for Your glory.

You are the star that shines brightly in my life and illuminates my path. I rely on You for my every decision. You direct my life.

My fist often clinches tightly, holding on to the things that are destroying me. I want to do things my way, when it is so clear that Your way is best. Give me the strength to let go and let You take over.

You only care about my well-being. You are trustworthy, and yes I do trust You. You have given me all of You and I now give You all of me.

I Love You

Lord,

You are faithful and true. I can count on You always. I am forever Yours. No matter what my circumstances are, I will trust You. Your presence is my joy.

I am completely and utterly lost without You. I rely on You alone for my daily sustenance, and You always come through, in Your time.

You alone know what is best for me. You can do no wrong and Your ways are perfect. Therefore I will not question the happenings in my life. Instead of wondering why, I will praise You and be glad.

I Love You

Lord,

Help me to not anticipate. I want to keep my eyes open wide for the opportunities You send my way, and I want to be a willing and available vessel for You.

Long before You created me, I existing in Your mind. You knew me before You made me. Your love for me is perfect and unshakable. My love for You grows with each new day.

Your presence is the gift that I long for. Unshackle me from the weight of this world. Free my mind so that I may focus on You.

All day long I think of You. You are at the top of my mind. You are my priority. You have won my heart and I will never let You go.

I Love You

Lord,

You are the only one who can wipe my slate clean. With each new day, You give me a fresh start: a new chance to make a difference. Guide me to the right choices, and give me the courage to choose rightly.

I thank You for Your unconditional love. No matter what I do, still You love me. I will be loyal to You forever.

The more I know You, the more You amaze me. Yes, You are an amazing God; worthy of my best! I give You my past, my present and my future. I give You my time and my treasure. All that I have is Yours.

My ultimate goal is to bring You joy. My desire is Your will fulfilled.

I Love You

Lord,

You have turned my sorrows into joy! I so often allow my mind to be overrun with so many things. But You remind me that the victory has already been won for me.

Quiet my mind and still my soul. Allow me to hear Your voice clearly and to obey You fully.

This world promises much, but delivers little. The trinkets this world has to offer are not worthy to be compared to the riches in glory that You have stored up for me.

Every day and all day I choose You. I will not let another steal my heart, for it belongs to You alone.

I Love You

Lord,

You are my hiding place. I will trust in You always. I will not fear.

When I rise in the morning You are there to greet me. I reach out and grab Your hand. You hold me close, and together we walk, hand in hand.

Your presence is the object of my fascination. You are who I live for, and You are always on my mind.

If only I could understand why You love me so. If only I could grasp the depth of Your great love for me. Alas, I will abandon my need to know and accept You as an infant accepts what comes: in complete and pure faith.

I Love You

Lord,

You are in control. I will not be afraid. Even when the enemy stalks me, I shall not be moved.

Your word is firmly planted within me. Weeds and thorns will not take their place! You are my King and I serve only You.

Why should I run in fear? Why should I hide when trouble surrounds me? I have the great Waymaker on my side. You clear the path beneath my feet.

I will always look to You for my help. You are my lover, and I am enraptured with You.

I Love You

Lord,

Your mercy is legendary. Though I have sinned against You, You keep no record of it.

Your humility is beyond compare. You are great and mighty—the designer of all things. There will never be another like You, yet You are content to walk with me.

I am Your servant. Use me and guide me along Your perfect path. You have prepared the way before me. You have ordered my steps. Give me the courage and strength to stay on Your narrow road.

With You in my life I lack nothing. Without You, I have nothing.

Your word is my food, and Your spirit quenches my thirst. You are my passion.

I Love You

Lord,

You are the love my life and the song of my heart. I pledge my life, my heart and my soul to You.

Shelter me from the evils of this world. Protect me. Make my mind clear and focus my attention on eternal things.

Illuminate Your perfect path before me. Refresh me from Your ever flowing river of life.

You are my singular focus and my reason for living. Continue to grant me the grace to follow You completely.

I praise Your holy name with all that is in me. May I lift You up in all that I do.

I Love You

Lord,

Thank You for Your compassion. Your love and Your kindness draw me closer to You. You bring sparkle and radiance to my life. Without You, I would cease to exist.

Why, O God are You so attracted to me? Your kindness never ceases and You never cease to amaze me! You welcome me with open arms, and You have forgotten my transgressions.

You are beyond compare. I Love You with a strong and unending love. You teach me new and exciting things every day.

Your mercy showers down upon me like a waterfall. It never stops. Continue Your cleansing work in my heart and mind. I am Yours forever.

I Love You

Lord,

I am in love with You. I am enraptured by the very sound of Your name. You love me with a perfect love.

You are the Master of my soul and the architect of my life. My destiny is in Your hands; right where it belongs. I will trust You completely with my past, and honor You with my present and my future.

Help me to trust and obey. I know that You will never wrong me, and I am safe following You.

Lead me in the way that is right and perfect for me. I pledge You my love and loyalty both now and forever.

I Love You

Lord,

Walking with You is a joy and a thrill. I am eager to see what new surprises You have in store for me today.

You are the great God of the universe, with billions of galaxies at Your command; and yet You care for my every need.

I will trust and love You completely because You deserve nothing less. I offer You everything that I am, so that You can mold me into everything You desire.

My obsession is to know You. You have made Yourself completely accessible and available to me, and I will take full advantage of Your great generosity.

I Love You

Lord,

Darkness and despair shall not overtake me. Evil will not have its say in my life. You have refreshed my soul and given me joy and peace. I will follow You.

No matter what my circumstance are—I will refuse to walk by sight. I will rest peacefully each night, for I am certain of your promises.

All the days of my life will be spent rendering praise, glory and honor to You. You have captivated my soul, and my hope rests in no other.

Your love has conquered my fears. Your amazing grace has overcome me. My soul is in Your hands and I will walk and reign with You forever.

I Love You

Lord,

You are my life. I am eternally dedicated to You. I have exchanged my will for Yours. Lead me along Your perfect path.

Wherever You are is where I want to be. I want to share in Your vision and help You accomplish Your dreams.

Give me the desire to serve You whole-heartedly. Change my mind so that it will be in alignment with Yours.

I look forward to our brilliant future together, and I want to begin that future now. You have given me life everlasting and I will use this great gift to uplift Your name throughout eternity.

I Love You

PART

②

HOW TO PRAY

PART ②

HOW TO PRAY

HOW DO WE PRAY WITH PURPOSE?

In the sixth chapter of the book of Matthew, we find what many have affectionately come to know as *"The Lord's Prayer."* It is, in fact, the Lord's *example* of how we should pray. It is His model of prayer. It's an example of the kinds of things we should pray for and about.

> *But thou, when thou prayest, enter into thy closet, and when thou hast shut thy door, pray to thy Father which is in secret; and thy Father which seeth in secret shall reward thee openly.* (Matthew 6:6)

God wants us to find a quiet place where we can pray to Him intimately and in private.

> *But when ye pray, use not vain repetitions, as the heathen do: for they think that they shall be heard for their much speaking. Be not ye therefore like unto them: for your Father knoweth what things ye have need of, before ye ask Him.* (Matthew 6:7-8)

God does not delight in long winded prayers that are said solely for the benefit of favor from others. Likewise,

He does not delight in prayers that are merely recited repetitiously and read or uttered without true conviction. Instead He desires us to have a real and personal relationship with Him. In fact, He already knows what we need - before we ask!

> *After this manner therefore pray ye: Our Father*
> *which art in heaven, Hallowed be thy name.*
> (Matthew 6:9)

Here Jesus is saying that we should praise God when we come to Him in prayer..

When we pray we acknowledge that we are addressing the one true eternal God. He alone is holy.

> *Thy kingdom come. Thy will be done in earth,*
> *as it is in heaven.* (Matthew 6:10)

Here Jesus is saying that we should surrender completely to God.

The word used for kingdom is the word *rule*. The Kingdom of God is the rule of God. In Luke 17:21, Jesus taught that "...the kingdom of God is within you." In fact, for the Christian, God has set up His kingdom in our heart. Therefore the kingdom of God is within and God himself is the King (ruler) of that kingdom.

If God has in fact set up His kingdom in our heart and He is our supreme King, then His will will be done in and through us. We will follow His will without question, trusting that He knows best.

Give us this day our daily bread. (Matthew 6:11)

Here Jesus is saying that we should bring our needs to God.

In this way, we continually acknowledge that God is the sole supplier of all our needs.

And forgive us our debts, as we forgive our debtors.
(Matthew 6:12)

Here Jesus is saying that we should have an attitude of humility and forgiveness.

We desire that God will forgive us of all our wrongs. In the same way, we are to forgive others who have wronged us.

And lead us not into temptation,
but deliver us from evil: (Matthew 6:13a)

Here Jesus is saying that God is the one who will keep us from all harm.

We pray that God will steer us clear of anything that will take off track or lead us away from following Him.

For thine is the kingdom, and the power,
and the glory, forever. Amen. (Matthew 6:13b)

Here Jesus is saying that everything revolves around God.

We acknowledge that God is all powerful and worthy of our worship.

When Christ gave us an example on how we ought to pray, He chose to do it in just 66 words. Remarkable.

No 500 word essay. Not even a hundred words. Short and sweet.

This is Jesus' example of how we ought to pray.

So, what is prayer?

Some say that prayer is talking to God. Still others say that prayer is communicating *with* God. While both of these answers are true, prayer is so much more. Prayer is *connecting* with God. In fact, prayer is what connects the heart of man to the heart of His Creator.

Keeping An Open Line.

Like an open wifi connection, we should keep our channel open to God at all times.

The Bible says that we should "pray without ceasing" 1 Thes. 5:17 KJV. The NIV reads "pray continually".

This means that we should maintain an open line of communication with the Lord. The truth is, we should be talking to Him all day long. Day in, day out; and all throughout the day - we are seeking His advice and listening out for His direction. He is our tour guide through life. Jesus already passed this way before! We can trust His leading!

We are carrying on a continuous conversation with our Lord. He is a true Friend indeed, and He is always with those who love Him.

There is a difference between *praying continually* and *praying with purpose*. Praying with purpose means that we set aside a specific block of time to pray to the Lord. Meanwhile we shut out all other distractions that the world may have to offer. *Praying without ceasing (praying continually)* means we keep our channel tuned into God throughout the day, with a constant stream of back and forth communication.

HOW LONG SHOULD I PRAY?

Admittedly this seems to be a trick question. On one hand the Bible teaches that we should pray without ceasing. On the other hand when Jesus gave us His example on how we should pray He used only 66 words! I've clocked it and that prayer takes a mere 27 seconds to recite.

Jesus himself says that your prayer time should be relatively short (Matt 6:7). Personally, I dedicate 15 minutes each morning to purposeful prayer. I then spend the rest of the day continually communing with Him.

DON'T FORGET WHERE GOD LIVES.

For the believer, God lives within our heart. It is easy to lose sight of this fact when we see believers looking "up to heaven" when they acknowledge God. I sometimes do this out of sheer habit.

The truth is God lives inside of us and when we pray to Him we are praying to 'the God who lives within us.'

Those who don't know Christ spend their day talking and thinking to themselves. Those who know Christ spend their day talking to Him. He alone is the source for life's most important answers.

HOW CAN I COME TO KNOW CHRIST?

Great question! Let's take a look together in the next section.

PART

③

THE GOSPEL OF JESUS

PART ③

THE GOSPEL OF JESUS

The story of our redemption by our great and mighty redeemer, Jesus Christ, began well before the world was framed, and before man was made. Let's take a look at the beautiful and fantastic story of our salvation.

GOD AND THE ANGELS IN HEAVEN

The Bible teaches that God created the Angels in heaven before He created the world, and before He created man. We know this, because God says that the Angels "shouted for joy" when God created the earth (Job 38:4-8).

LUCIFER TURNS AGAINST GOD

Lucifer (now known as the devil and satan) was one of the angels created by God. God says that Lucifer was created perfect in both wisdom and beauty. He was in Eden, the garden of God. His clothing was adorned with the finest jewels, and created with the finest gold. Lucifer was a mighty angelic guardian. He was blameless. But one day he turned against God. Why would he do such a thing? For the same reasons we do. He was filled with pride because of his beauty and wealth, and he forgot God. He looked only to himself. (Ezekiel 28:11-17). Today, more and more people are looking everywhere but to God for their help.

LUCIFER THROWN OUT OF HEAVEN

As Lucifer's heart became more and more twisted, he thought that he should be in control of heaven! He felt that he could do a much better job than his own Creator! As crazy as that may sound, many of us believe the same thing. Although we acknowledge God in some ways, we don't turn our lives over to Him, so that He can have complete control. Although God created us, we often think we know what's best.

Somehow, in his sly way, the devil convinced a third of the angels that he should be the next President of Heaven, and they sought to overthrow God! And so it was that war broke out in heaven. The angel Michael and the angels under his command fought against the devil and his angels. Of course Satan lost the battle, and he was thrown out of heaven, and was cast down to the earth (Revelation 12:7-9).

WHY DIDN'T GOD SIMPLY DESTROY SATAN?

God loves all of His creation and He desires that His creation love Him in return. But He will not force us to love Him. We are all given the freedom to choose to love Him, only if we want to. If we don't want to love God and serve Him, then we don't have to (Joshua 24:15).

Satan made his choice. He chose NOT to serve God, but to follow His own way. Satan even convinced many of the angels that his way was best. Although it was a terrible choice, the Lord still recognized Satan's choice, and allowed him to prove his lie. If God had simply zapped Satan and his rebelling army of angels right there, then the rest of the angels might have served God out of fear. God doesn't want anyone to serve Him because they are afraid of Him. Only tyrants rule that way. God wants us to serve Him because we love Him (1 John 4:16-18).

Of course God could have put a stop to Satan before he

was able to convince a third of the angels to rebel. But God cannot go against His own nature. By nature, God is just, and He offers us a choice. God tells us which way to choose, but He allows us to make the choice. Even though He knows that the choice we make may harm us, or even kill us.

Imagine you were on a game show and the show's host asked you to pick a door for your grand prize. He tells you: "Behind door number one is a brand new car and a million dollars cash, and behind door number two you will find a pit full of poisonous snakes." Of course, you would pick door number one! But on a TV game show, you have to guess the right door. In the real world, God tells you which door to choose! God says, "Today I have given you a choice between life and death, between blessings and curses. I call on heaven and earth to witness the choice you make. Oh, that you may choose life...!" Deuteronomy 30:19.

GOD CREATES MAN

God made a decision to make a new creation. He would call His new creation "Man". So God created man in His own image (Genesis 1:27). God blessed the man and told him to "Multiply and fill the earth, and subdue it" (Genesis 1:28). God's plan was that mankind was to rule over the earth, and to do what was pleasing in God's sight.

GOD PLANTS A GARDEN FOR MAN

The Lord planted a wonderful garden in Eden, and He placed the man there. The garden contained all sorts of trees that produced delicious fruit. And at the center of the garden, God placed two trees: the Tree Of Life and the Tree of Knowledge of Good and Evil (Genesis 2:8,9).

The Bible goes on to say "The Lord God placed the man in the Garden of Eden to tend and care for it. But the Lord God gave him this warning 'You may freely eat any fruit in the garden, except fruit from the Tree of Knowledge Of Good and Evil. If you eat of its fruit you will surely die'" (Genesis 2:15-17).

Notice that God gave man freedom over the entire earth and everything in it. There were millions of things that man could do. But there was ONE thing that God said NOT to do. This was man's test. He could prove his devotion and loyalty to his Creator by simply obeying this one command.

GOD CREATES WOMAN

Afterward, God made woman. He took a rib from the side of man, and fashioned the woman from the man. This signified that the two (man and woman) would always be side by side, working together toward the fulfillment of God's destiny for them. God named the man Adam, and the woman Eve (Genesis 2:18-25).

THE FALL OF MAN

God created man as a perfect being. He was without any sin or guilt. But the devil came along and began trying to work some of his magic on God's new creation. If the devil could get man to rebel against God, then he would have even more followers! Since he couldn't steal heaven from God, maybe he could get a hold of God's prized possession: man!

And so, in the form of a serpent, the devil appeared to Eve. He convinced her that she could eat of the tree that God said not to eat from. He gave her a very convincing argument. Doubt began to fill her mind, and she eventually began to believe the devil's lies. She took a piece of the forbidden fruit, and ate it. She then took some of the fruit and gave it to her husband with her, and he ate it. Suddenly they realized what they had done, but it was too late. (Gen. 3:1-7)

You may be thinking, "what's the big deal? It's just a piece of fruit." But it was so much bigger than that. Adam and Eve had betrayed their loyalty to their Creator.

Let me ask you a question. How much does a person have to steal in order to be considered a thief? Let's say you invited me over to your house for supper. If I stole a $10 bill off your bathroom counter, would you consider me a thief? What if I only stole a dime? Either way, I'm still a thief, and you would no longer trust me in your home.

ADAM, THE AMBASSADOR OF MAN

God created Adam and Eve to live forever. However, God told Adam and Eve that if they ate from the forbidden tree, then they would surely die. As a result, death entered the human race. And the disease of disobedience (sin) entered the race as well. Since Adam was the ambassador of the human race, all people after him would be infected by the deadly virus called sin (Romans 5:12). Sin is simply disobedience to God (1 John 3:4).

MAN CHOOSES DEATH

When Adam and Eve chose to disobey God, they were choosing death instead of life. Ultimately, though, they felt ashamed of what they did. But God had already declared that death would be the result of their disobedience. And rightly so.

When doctors find cancer in the body, they have no choice but to get rid of it. If they don't it will spread, and corrupt everything in its path. Sin is like a cancer. God has to cut it off; or else it will have devastating affects. Look at the chaos Satan caused in heaven! Look how busy he is here on earth!

As we mentioned earlier, God created man to be immortal. But man chose death instead of life. After thousands of years, we still haven't gotten used to death. That's why there's so much grieving at funerals. Since the dawn of earth, billions of people have died. You would think that by now we would be used to death, and think of it as 'no big deal' or at least a natural process of life. But man cannot embrace the idea of death. We were not meant to die!

GOD PROVIDES A FREE GIFT

And so it was, after sin, mankind was now on death row. There is a debt that every man must pay. The debt you owe is your life. But, alas! God, in His tremendous love and mercy, has decided to pay the debt for you!

Suppose you committed a crime and were found guilty, and sentenced to death. Then, someone you don't even know offered to serve your sentence for you. You could choose to accept the sentence of death, or you could choose to accept the generous free gift from this stranger, who is offering to die in your place.

Well, such an offer has been extended to you. Only this offer is for your eternal soul. You can loose your soul eternally, or you can live forever—the choice is yours.

God sent His Son, Jesus Christ, to die for our sins, so that we would not have to die an eternal death. Those who accept the free gift that Christ offers will be granted eternal life. "For God so loved the world that He gave His only Son, so that everyone who believes in Him will not perish but have everlasting life." (John 3:16)

Jesus came to earth in the form of a baby, through a virgin named Mary (Matthew 1:18-24). He lived a perfect and sinless life on earth (Isaiah 53:7-9). And although He was without blame, He was crucified on a wooden cross, because we rejected Him (Matthew 27:32-56).

But the grave couldn't contain Christ! He was resurrected from the dead, three days after He was killed and buried (Matthew 28:1-10).

GOD'S PLAN FOR YOU

God desires that you be reconciled to Him. He made the HUGE first step, by paying your sin debt in full. You must acknowledge Christ as Lord, and turn to God. The Bible says "For the wages of sin is death, but the free gift of God is eternal life through Jesus Christ our Lord" (Romans 6:23). *This is called salvation.* Once we accept Christ, we are "saved" from death.

WHAT YOU MUST DO:

1. Recognize that the Lord loves you (John 3:16)

2. Recognize that you are a sinner, in need of the Savior, Jesus Christ. (Romans 3:23).

3. Recognize that your sin has separated you from God (Romans 6:23).

4. Recognize that Christ is the ONLY WAY to God (John 14:6).

5. You must receive Christ as your Lord and Savior (John 1:12; Ephesians 2:8,9).

Christ is waiting to come into your life and transform it! Jesus says, *"Look! Here I stand at the door and knock. If you hear me calling and open the door, I will come in, and we will share a meal as friends"* (Revelation 3:20).

The Lord is what you have been searching for to fill the void in your life. If you can hear the Lord knocking at the door of your heart, let Him in!

HOW TO BECOME
A CHRISTIAN

There is nothing greater than to live your life for Jesus Christ. If you are not a Christian, the Lord is calling you today! Will you listen to His call of salvation? Millions have already made a decision to live for Christ. If you feel the Lord tugging at your heart today, don't wait. Pray this prayer of deliverance:

Prayer: "Dear God, I know that I am a sinner, and I am truly sorry for my sins. I know that You sent Your Son Jesus Christ who died for my sins, and is now at Your side in Heaven. Please save me from my sins and purify my life. I choose to live my life for You 100%. I thank You for salvation and eternal life. In the name of Jesus Christ. Amen."

If you sincerely prayed that prayer you can rest assured that you are now a child of God! As a new Christian the devil will try to come against you with everything he can.

Be sure to:

- Find a Christian church that preaches Jesus.

- Connect with a Christian friend who can have Bible studies with you.

- Read your Bible daily (I recommend that you begin with the book of John) to learn more about Christ. You can even download a variety of free Bible Apps!

- Pray to the Lord daily and stay in constant communion with Him.

Remember, salvation is a free gift that the Lord has given you. Make Jesus Christ the Lord of your life by seeking His will and serving Him every day.

Being a Christian isn't popular. Jesus wasn't popular when He was on the earth, and He still isn't. But being a Christian is not about being popular. Once you know the truth, it is up to you what you do with it. But Christ says "If anyone acknowledges me publicly here on earth, I will openly acknowledge that person before my Father in heaven. But if anyone denies me here on earth, I will deny that person in heaven." Matthew 10:32, 33.

Being a Christian isn't easy. It's a straight and narrow road, and very few will walk it! The key to a successful Christian life is surrender. Those who choose to allow Christ to reign supreme in their lives, will experience great victory, as they live their lives in the center of God's will. As you realize that God only wants what is best for you, it becomes easier to surrender your will for His. Some well meaning folks (loved ones, friends, etc.) will try to discourage your walk with Christ. They will think you've gone off on the deep end. But if Christ was willing to die publicly for you, you ought to be willing to live publicly for Him. He's got no shame in claiming you as His child. You should have no shame in claiming Him as your Lord!

We pray that the Lord will bless your journey as you begin your walk with Him. For those who have wandered from the Lord—It's never too late to come back home! May the Lord richly bless you. Knolly & Josie Williams

---

Made in the USA
Coppell, TX
11 June 2021